Matthew 5:1–2
     And seeing the multitudes, He went up on a mountain, and
when He was seated His disciples came to Him. Then He
opened His mouth and taught them.

Matthew 5:3
     Blessed are the poor in spirit,
          For theirs is the kingdom of heaven.

Matthew 5:4
     Blessed are those who mourn,
          For they shall be comforted.

Matthew 5:5
Blessed are the meek,
For they shall inherit the earth.

Matthew 5:6
Blessed are those who hunger and thirst for righteousness,
For they shall be filled.

Matthew 5:7
Blessed are the merciful,
For they shall obtain mercy.

THE
BIBLE
VERSE
BOOK

THE
BIBLE
VERSE
BOOK

LaVonne Masters

THOMAS NELSON PUBLISHERS
Nashville

Published in Nashville, Tennessee, by Thomas Nelson,
Inc., and distributed in Canada by Lawson Falle, Ltd.,
Cambridge, Ontario.

Printed in the United States of America.

Library of Congress Cataloging-in-Publication Data

Masters, LaVonne.
    The Bible verse book / LaVonne Masters.
      p.   cm.
    Summary: Presents five steps to help children
memorize the Scriptures and understand and apply
those verses to their lives at home, at school, and
with their friends.
    ISBN 0-8407-3229-5
    1. Bible—Memorizing. 2. Christian education of
children.
    [1. Bible—Memorizing. 2. Christian life.] I. Title.
BS617.7.M37 1991
220'.07—dc20   91-7606
                                 CIP
                                 AC

Printed in the United States of America
1 2 3 4 5 6 7 — 96 95 94 93 92 91

To my cherished grandchildren

Jonathan David and Christie LaVonne Westerfield.

Special acknowledgment to

Kathy Dawson
for her skills in children's education
that made this edition possible.

Thank you.

CONTENTS

A NOTE TO PARENTS

I have had parents say to me numerous times, "I don't want to make my children rebellious by forcing them to attend church or making them read the Bible." However, when they are encouraged with the right spirit, I've never seen children become rebellious about going to church or learning the Word. It is the child who does not learn faithfulness in church attendance and a love for the Scriptures who has no foundation of values and will, in the end, become rebellious.

As parents, we want the very best for our children. We send them to school to learn. We teach our children habits for health and cleanliness. We do anything we can to help them become involved in the extracurricular activities of their choice: music, sports, hobbies, travel, computers.

The best way to guide our children spiritually is to live the way we expect our children to live. The best way to help our children learn to memorize and meditate on Scripture is for us to memorize and meditate on Scripture. If we are learning the teachings and principles with Scripture through Memorize and Meditate, and if we are consistently practicing these in our lives, our children will not depart from our spiritual training and will grow up to respect and revere us and the God we serve.

You will find the complete memorization and meditation program for adults in my book for adults, *Memorize and Meditate*. As you work through the five D's of the program—decide the method, determine the location, discover the content, draw the application, and do it—you can be available to help your children walk through the steps of the program. Learning the Scriptures as a family also gives the entire family an opportunity to better understand and encourage one another. Take time once a week to give each member of the family an opportunity to share what he is learning. Saturday nights or Sunday evenings are good times for this.

Take time to read through this book with your children, or at least to read it before they use it. Before your children begin to learn and use the five D's of Memorize and Meditate, help them choose a Bible translation that is appropriate for their age, yet try to choose one they will not quickly outgrow. The five D's for Kids' Memorize and Meditate are the same as the five D's for the adults' program.

Decide the Method

Help your children choose the one method of memorization they are most comfortable with. Remember, memorizing is easy for kids. Their minds are fresh and quick. And the most common way children learn information and facts is by repetition. So this should be a guaranteed method of learning. However, the other methods are equally as valid, and sometimes very helpful.

Two methods of memorization that are especially helpful for younger children are association and the use of cassette tapes. Association involves relating each verse to a picture you or your child draws. Keep the picture simple.

For children who enjoy listening to cassettes, record portions of Scripture so they can listen to the tapes throughout the day. The children will not only learn Scripture but they will have the reassurance of hearing Mom or Dad's voice during the day. And if they play the Scripture tapes just before they go to sleep at night, they'll sleep better.

Determine the Location

You may want to help your children determine the portion of Scripture they memorize. I've included two lists of passages: one in chapter 4, pages 49–50, and one, which is arranged according to age, at the back of the book. It is less work for you if all your children are working on the same Scriptures at the same time. However, one child may need a different Scripture because of his or her specific need for encouragement or instruction, or because he or she is not at the same level as the other children. Be sensitive to this and help each child determine the number of verses he or she can comfortably memorize each week.

Discover the Content

When researching key words with preschoolers, you may not want to use a dictionary. Instead, use examples to teach word meanings. To teach the meaning for the word *kind,* for example, you might demonstrate politeness. If a sibling takes advantage of them, show them how to be "kind" in return.

Simplify thoughts and explanations for each age level. Take an active part in sharing and discussing the verses with your children so they learn to meditate on their own level.

Draw the Application

As your children begin to apply the Scriptures they are memorizing to their lives, prompt their creative thinking by asking questions:

What do you think about this verse?

What do you feel about this verse?

How can this verse fit into (apply to) your life?

Open-ended questions, such as these, affirm your children's ideas and inspire creative thinking. This is a good time for you as a parent to add new ideas in the discussion with your children.

Use every opportunity during the week to point out, in a casual manner, how the verses they are learning relate to their lives. Incorporate applications into your prayer time with each child. Ask God to help you be alert to living object lessons. And trust that the Holy Spirit will enlighten your children's minds to the truth of the Word for application to their lives. The Holy Spirit speaks and makes Scripture real to children too.

Do It

It is important for you to help your children relax and enjoy memorization and meditation so they will have a desire to continue the program through their adult years and someday help their children memorize and meditate. As you walk through the steps together, consider these additional helps:

1. Use a five-day schedule. On the weekend give Memorize and Meditate a rest unless an opportune moment occurs for casually teaching the meaning or application of a verse your children are working on.

2. *Use incentives*. Incentives are not bribery but rewards to reassure your children that their behavior merits value at home. As long as rewards are necessary, feel comfortable about using them to reinforce your values to your children. Make the rewards appropriate for the number of verses your children learn and for their specific ages. The following list gives several suggestions:

AGES 2 TO 5

A sticker	M & M candy	Cookie
Ice cream	Help mom bake	Coloring book
Stay up later	Inexpensive toy	New book
A picnic	Money for whatever	Trip to zoo
First Bible	Shopping trip with mom or dad	

AGES 6 TO 12

Special bike ride	Permission to go to friend's
Lunch with mom and dad	New book or cassette
New clothing item	Slumber party at home

Money for almost whatever
Attend a major-league game with parents
Toy model—like electric train and accessories

AGES 13 TO 18

New "fad" item	Friend for overnight
Strong's Concordance	Money for almost whatever
New book or cassette	Family car for one day
Item for collection	Leather Bible

Privilege to stay up late one night (at home!)

Dad or mom will do one of their chores
Dinner with dad or mom at an exclusive restaurant

3. Relax with your children. Sit in a comfortable chair or lie on the bed with younger children as they meditate on Scriptures (children six or seven years and older may want to meditate alone). Listen to them talk out loud about the Scriptures they are learning.

4. Keep a positive attitude about Memorize and Meditate. Sometimes children will make mistakes when saying their verses for you. When this happens, repeat the verse in the correct form without drawing attention to the error. This encourages communication and does not dampen their spirits.

There are fifty-two weeks in a year and children attend school for thirteen years, kindergarten through twelfth grade. If a child learns just one verse of Scripture a week for thirteen years, he will learn 676 verses by the time he graduates from high school. With a little more effort, your children can learn the entire book of Mark, which has 678 verses, or they can learn a combination of several passages and chapters:

The Sermon on the Mount	**111 verses**
Ephesians	**155 verses**
Philippians	**104 verses**

1 Timothy	113 verses
James	108 verses
1 John	<u>105 verses</u>
	696 verses

Planting this amount of Scripture in your children's minds will help them develop positive actions and attitudes. If you help and encourage them to memorize and meditate on the Scriptures, and if you are a living example before them, you will, indeed, be "training up" your children in the way they should go.

CHAPTER 1

The Beginning

In the beginning there was God. Then God created the world and all the plants and animals in it. Finally, the Creator looked around and saw that everything was good, but decided to make one more creature. "All these other things are very nice," He may have said. "But I would like to have something in this world to love, something who will love Me." So, He reached down in the dust and made a new creature. The new creature was called "man." And that is how we came to be!

God loves us very much. And He wants us to love Him. But how can we love someone back who we can't see with our eyes? We can't do the things we would do for our other friends. We can't give Him a hug. We can't send Him a birthday present, even if we knew when His birthday is! We can't even bake Him a cake or some chocolate chip cookies. Yet God gives us so much. What can we give Him in return? Jesus, Himself, gave us the answer in the book of Matthew:

You shall love the Lord your God with all your heart, with all your soul, and with all your mind.
Matthew 22:37

When you give God your heart, soul, and mind, you learn more about Him. If God were one of your friends from school, you would want to get to know Him better by spending time with Him.

What does He like? What makes Him happy? What makes Him laugh?

You learn these things from your friends by listening to them and talking with them. You ask them questions. Though you may spend time with them in a group, you also spend time alone with them. It's much easier to get to know someone if there aren't other people around.

"So," you might say, "how can I get to know someone I can't see? I can see my friends and talking with them is so much easier than talking to someone I can't see."

You can get to know God by reading the Bible and understanding what it says. Two ways to do this are by memorizing and meditating on God's Word.

How do you feel about memorizing things? You may be thinking, "I can't memorize anything." But, the fact is, we memorize what we want to remember. You probably can tell me your friends' telephone numbers, or maybe the batting averages of your favorite baseball players. These are things you want to know.

A boy named Matt thought he couldn't spell. He found that when he worked on memorizing the words, he could get 100 percent on his spelling tests. He made flash cards of his words and his mother quizzed him. Sometimes he put the words in stories or sentences. He found a way to use them during class. Doing all these things helped him to go from a "C" in spelling to an "A" in one report card period. It was hard work, but he felt good about himself.

God will give you the power to learn His Word. Ask Him. Just think, if you started to memorize Bible verses in kindergarten and learned one verse each week until you graduated from high school, you would memorize *676 verses!*

When you memorize Scripture, you store in your mind stories and truths about God, His personality, and the way He relates to people. This gives you something to think about and can also help you when you pray to God.

When you think about and talk with God, you are meditating. Most people know what the word *memorize* means, but not everyone knows the meaning of *meditate* or how to do it. Let's see what the word means when it's used in the Bible.

The Old Testament is written in the Hebrew language. Two of the Hebrew words in the Old Testament for *meditate* are *hagah* and *siyach*. *Hagah* (pronounced haw-gaw') is used in Joshua 1:8: "This Book of the Law shall not depart from your mouth, but you shall meditate in it day and night, that you may observe to do according to all that is written in it." The word *meditate* in this verse means talking quietly with yourself.

The second Hebrew word for *meditate, siyach* (pronounced see-akh), can be found in Psalm 119:15: "I will meditate on Your precepts, and contemplate Your ways." Here, *meditate* means to think about and pray.

In chapters 3—7, you'll learn five D's to help you to learn more about Memorize and Meditate:

Decide How
Determine Where
Discover What
Draw Out Why
Do It

But before you start, there are a few things you need to know.

CHAPTER 2

Before You Start

Before you start to memorize and meditate, you'll need an idea of what's to come and a few tools that will make the rest of the book easier to use. You will learn how to quickly look up Scripture verses in the Bible. And you will learn how to use an index card for meditating.

The Preview

Chapter 3, "Decide How"

In this chapter, I'll give you all the secrets I know about how to memorize. You'll learn about several different ways to memorize. And as you're reading this book, you'll be able to try each of them and use the ones that work best for you.

Chapter 4, "Determine Where"

This chapter will help you choose verses from the Bible to memorize. It contains a checklist with some Bible verses I thought you might enjoy. It gives you some idea of what these verses are about and where to find them. When you finish memorizing your verses for one section, write the date in this book!

Chapter 5, "Discover What"

This chapter may seem to you like some of the work you do at school. (I heard you groaning.

We'll have none of that now. You might even enjoy this.) You'll use a dictionary to discover what the important words in your verse mean. I'll talk about some other steps that you can use to help understand your verse.

Chapter 6, "Draw Out Why"

This is the most exciting part. You'll be looking for ways that your verses fit with your life.

Chapter 7, "Do It"

In this chapter, I'll review what you've learned. There will be a schedule to help you decide how much to memorize each week. And I'll give you some final tools to help you keep your memorization and meditation plan going.

The Cards

I don't mean your birthday cards or your baseball cards! The cards I'm talking about are cards that will help you review the parts of the Bible that you've memorized. If you've ever tried to memorize an oral report for school, you will know that it helps to break your report down into little chunks. The same thing goes for long sections of Scripture.

You will need some 3″ x 5″ index cards and a file box in which to keep them. You can use a different color card for each section of the Bible you

are memorizing, but it is not necessary. Decorate your file box to make it yours. You will be using it for a long time, so make it important to you. You will also need divider cards to separate your index cards into groups of verses. These should have labels so you can write the title of each book/chapter you are studying. Before writing on the index cards, make a label for your book and chapter. In this book I will be using the Beatitudes to help practice the skills we are talking about. (The Beatitudes are words that Jesus gave His disciples during the Sermon on the Mount about the kinds of people that will receive blessings.) You will find these in the fifth chapter of Matthew. So write on your divider label "Matthew 5."

You will need to have your index cards and box before you finish reading this book, because we will do one card together.

The Bible

In chapter 4, I'll talk about some of the different versions of the Bible that you might use. Right now, I'm going to have you look up the Beatitudes we were talking about before. Get your family Bible or the closest one you can find for this exercise.

Open your Bible to the book of Matthew. Yes, that's in the New Testament, which is near the last part of your Bible. Once you have Matthew, look for a large number "5." You may have to turn a few pages before you find it. After you've found the large number "5," look for a little number "3." Congratulations! You have just found Matthew 5:3, the first Beatitude.

You can also use the headings at the top of the page like we did when we looked up the verse in our *Nelson's Children's Bible*. Your Bible page might look like one of the two pictured on the following page.

You will be writing six things on each card:

1) the verse number to help you find it again
2) the verse itself

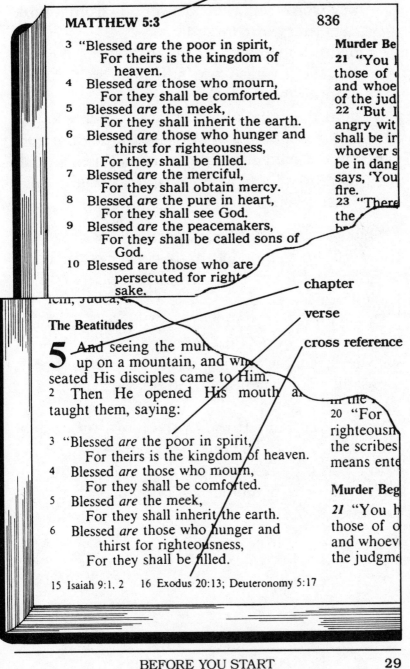

reference headings

MATTHEW 5:3   836

3 "Blessed *are* the poor in spirit,
  For theirs is the kingdom of
    heaven.
4 Blessed *are* those who mourn,
  For they shall be comforted.
5 Blessed *are* the meek,
  For they shall inherit the earth.
6 Blessed *are* those who hunger and
    thirst for righteousness,
  For they shall be filled.
7 Blessed *are* the merciful,
  For they shall obtain mercy.
8 Blessed *are* the pure in heart,
  For they shall see God.
9 Blessed *are* the peacemakers,
  For they shall be called sons of
    God.
10 Blessed are those who are
     persecuted for right
       sake.

Murder Be
21 "You
those of
and whoe
of the jud
22 "But I
angry wit
shall be ir
whoever s
be in dang
says, 'You
fire.
23 "There
the
h

chapter

verse

cross reference

iem, Judea,

The Beatitudes

5 And seeing the mul
  up on a mountain, and wh
seated His disciples came to Him.
2 Then He opened His mouth a
taught them, saying:

3 "Blessed *are* the poor in spirit,
  For theirs is the kingdom of heaven.
4 Blessed *are* those who mourn,
  For they shall be comforted.
5 Blessed *are* the meek,
  For they shall inherit the earth.
6 Blessed *are* those who hunger and
    thirst for righteousness,
  For they shall be filled.

in the
20 "For
righteousn
the scribes
means ente

Murder Beg

21 "You h
those of o
and whoev
the judgme

15 Isaiah 9:1, 2   16 Exodus 20:13; Deuteronomy 5:17

3) key words and their definitions from a Bible dictionary or concordance
4) definitions of key words from a regular dictionary (in case you still need help understanding the word)
5) your thoughts about what this verse is saying or a clever way you used to memorize it
6) quotes from other books (sometimes it helps to read what other people thought your verse meant)

Now get your first index card and write "Matthew 5:3" in the top left-hand corner of the card. Then, copy the verse exactly as it appears in your Bible onto the card.

Don't forget capital letters and punctuation! This will be important when you memorize. If you have trouble writing small enough to fit the verse on your card, ask one of your parents to help.

You've just gone through the first two steps of memorization. Keep your index cards nearby, because you'll be using them as you learn the different methods of memorization and as you begin to meditate on the verses you memorize.

CHAPTER 3

Decide How

"How could I remember all those verses?" "I'm just not good at remembering things." If either of these thoughts popped into your mind, then this chapter is for you. I'm going to give you five different ways to help you remember Bible verses. You can use one or more of these methods when you memorize your own verses. For right now, try each method with Matthew 5:3. Later, when you do your own verses, pick the ones you like the best.

Method #1: REPEAT REPEAT REPEAT

Most people use repetition when they memorize.

There are several steps to this method.

Read the verse several times.

Find Matthew 5:3 in your Bible. You can use your card since you have already written it. Read the verse at least three times so it sticks in your mind like chewing gum. Try to be in a quiet place, so you can think. Your bedroom or a quiet place outdoors is a better choice than a crowded playground or a football game.

Now, *see* the verse in your mind.

Look closely at your verse, then try to picture it. Did you notice the big words? How about the periods? Do you know which words have capital letters? Do that now with Matthew 5:3. Make sure you always use the same Bible from which to memorize so that the picture of that verse will always be the same in your mind.

Talk the verse.

When you are talking out loud, you are using both your voice and your ears. It may seem strange to you at first, but this helps you learn twice as fast. Say the verse out loud. Try whispering it. If you're not in a library, try shouting it. See what works best for you.

Write the verse three times.

You won't need to write out every verse you memorize, but if you're stuck on a verse, this can help. Use a sheet of paper other than your index card to do this. (You can use the space below to write Matthew 5:3.)

Exodus 20:8

Remember the Sabbath day, to
  keep it holy.
Remember the Sabbath day, to
  keep it holy.
Remember the S

Stretch your mind.

Just as your body needs exercise at recess and P.E., your mind also needs a workout. Start those brain push-ups: 1, 2, 3, 4. You can use this exercise.

Try to remember as much of the verse as you can before checking yourself in the Bible. Try to do a little more each time. By stretching your mind this way, you're doing the same thing for your mind that the push-ups do for your body. You will get more out of it each time you exercise.

Learn every word.

You haven't learned a verse if you haven't learned it perfectly. Take an index card. Place it over the verse. Move it down one line at a time as you say it. Cover what you're saying. Then, uncover it to check. *No peeking!*

Take a recess.

You use recesses at school to put space between subjects that you're learning. Use this for learning Bible verses too. Say your verse three times. Then, take a break. Later, say it three more times. Take another break, and say it again three times. How long a break should you take? It could be just a few minutes like a regular recess, or you could say your verse before school, after school, and before you go to bed for your three study times.

Finish what you start.

To feel good about what you are doing, you'll need to finish the verses you've started. I was one of those kids who got excited about a project and worked hard for a while, but then I lost interest and stuck it away in a drawer. By the time I grew up, I had many drawers of unfinished projects.

One thing that has helped me to finish things now that I'm an adult is to reward myself for finishing a project. My reward might be as simple as calling a friend or reading a favorite book. I give myself bigger rewards when I finish a bigger project, such as when I memorize a whole chapter of the Bible. Maybe you can work out a reward system with your parents. To help you keep track of what you've already memorized, I've included a checklist in chapter 4. You can put the date in the last column when you've memorized one of the Bible sections listed.

Method #2: FORM ACRONYMS

An acronym is made when you take the first letters of a group of words and make a new word. For example, most schools have a P.T.A. This acronym stands for the words *Parent–Teacher Association*. You can use this method for memorizing tough Bible lists too.

Pick out the key words in your verse. I'll use the first of the Beatitudes, Matthew 5:3:

Blessed are the poor in spirit,
For theirs is the kingdom of heaven.

The key words are *blessed, poor, spirit, kingdom,* and *heaven*. The acronym would be BPSKH. If memorizing this strange new word isn't enough, you can also create a new sentence using these letters. In the space below, list at least five words you know that begin with "B," "P," "S,"

"K," and "H." Then, choose a word from each list to make a sentence. For instance, Bears Paint Silly Kangaroo Houses.

B	P	S	K	H
Bears	Paint	Silly	Kangaroo	Houses
1.	1.	1.	1.	1.
2.	2.	2.	2.	2.
3.	3.	3.	3.	3.
4.	4.	4.	4.	4.
5.	5.	5.	5.	5.

You can add your favorite sentence from above to the back of your index card.

Method #3: ASSOCIATE

See a silly picture in your mind that goes along with your verse. For instance, you might imagine yourself with a see-through crown on your head or as a poor king or queen dressed in robes with holes in them to help you see in your mind a literal picture of "poor in spirit." Take a minute now to draw what comes into your mind when you think of the words of Matthew 5:3. (Use the space provided.) You can make the picture as silly as possible to help you remember. But if you're spending more time trying to think up a silly picture for your verse than you are memorizing that verse, you probably don't need to use this method.

Association works well with descriptive passages, such as Ephesians 6:10–20, which gives a picture of what it is to "take up the whole armor of God," or Romans 8:31–39, which gives a picture of God's everlasting love. You'll see how much easier it is to remember verses, such as Ephesians 6:14, "Stand therefore, having girded your waist with truth," when you imagine yourself wearing an oversized belt made of the word TRUTH.

Method #4: RECORD ON CASSETTE

If you have a tape recorder, record yourself reading the Beatitudes. Then, play it back over and over again to check yourself. You could record one verse several times or recite a whole section. If you don't want to listen to your own voice, have your parents or one of your friends record the verses for you. If you have a tape recorder, go ahead and try this now. The best time to play the tape back is right before you go to sleep at night. This is when your mind can work best without being distracted by other thoughts.

Method #5: MAKE UP SONGS

Take the words of the verse you are learning and put it to a song you already know. How about singing the Beatitudes to the tune of "Yankee Doodle" or Psalm 24 to "When the Saints Go Marching In"?

If you can't think of a song to fit your verse, make one up. It doesn't have to be a great melody. It just has to help you remember the verse. Teach your song to someone else or put homemade instruments with it to really help the words stick with you. On a bad day this can make you laugh. See if you can sing Matthew 5:3 to the tune of "Yankee Doodle" now. You will probably run out of words before you run out of music, but you can always add the rest of the Beatitudes later.

Now that I've told you all my secrets for memorizing Bible verses, you'll need to find the verses you want to memorize.

1. Blessed are the poor in spir - it

CHAPTER 4

Determine Where

How do you decide what to memorize in the Bible? You can use what I call The Doctor Doolittle Method. Whenever the doctor wanted to begin a voyage, he would get his chart book and a pin. He'd close his eyes, open the book and stick the pin in a page. Wherever the pin stuck, that's where the ship would go.

This method of memorization has two major problems. First, it puts too many holes in an already holy book. Second, picking a place to begin at random is like reading only the middle of a book. You miss what comes before and what comes after your verse.

Another way to memorize is by using what I call the freight train method. This means that you start at Genesis and memorize each verse, straight through to Revelation. Although this allows you always to know what comes before your verse, it has problems too. By using this method, you would be very, very old by the time you got to Jesus in the New Testament.

So how do we find out where to start? Pray to God. He knows what is going on in your life and will guide you to what will help you the most in the Bible. God is there when you make the base-ball team. God knows when you've done badly on a test or feel lonely. God's right there beside you when you have a bright idea. He cares for you. He will guide you to what you need to learn. You probably won't hear a voice saying, "Brian, read the Beatitudes." But you might have a Sunday school lesson on them or hear a song about them or have someone ask you if you've read them.

Sometimes God is not that direct. So if you're still not sure what to memorize, choose a story that you've always loved, maybe one of the para-bles of Jesus. (These are found in the books of Matthew, Mark, Luke, or John.) You could ask your parents to tell you their favorite chapter in the Bible. Don't be afraid to talk to your parents or a friend about what you're doing. God often speaks through people we care about and who love us.

Once you've decided where to start, choose a section of Scripture—several verses from one chapter, not individual verses from several loca-tions. This will help you find the verses you have memorized later. It is easier to find something again the more time you spend with it. Start with a small section of verses. Do not try to memorize a whole book on your first try.

I've listed some verses on the next few pages. If there are too many choices for you, try one of the following passages: Psalm 1, Psalm 23, Matthew 6:9–13, or Luke 10:30–37.

Don't let large sections of verses scare you. Memorize each section one verse at a time. Always try to quote the whole passage along with each new verse you learn. Say verse one; then verses one and two; then verses one, two, and three.

You can use the topics in the chart on pages 49–50 to help you find verses that may relate to what is going on in your life right now. Perhaps you've looked outside recently and wondered why God created the sun, moon, and stars. If so, you'll want to memorize and meditate on the creation story. Or if you're afraid you won't make the baseball team, you may want to read a passage about trusting God.

After you have memorized a particular set of verses, you can write the date of completion in the last column in the chart. I've also included a list of verses for Memorize and Meditate, which is arranged according to age groups, at the back of this book. If you want to find passages that are particularly good for people your age to memorize, you can look there.

Make Your Own Choice

Before you learn how to meditate on Scriptures, see how the methods of memorization that you learned in chapter 3 work when you choose your own verse from one of the lists on pages 49–50 or 89–96. Remember this verse, because you'll be meditating on it later.

BIBLE SECTION CHECKLIST

TOPIC	BIBLE CHAPTER AND VERSE	DATE COMPLETED
The Creation Story	Genesis 1:1—2:4	
The First Rainbow	Genesis 9:8–17	
The Commandments	Exodus 20:1–17 Matthew 22:36–40 John 13:34, 35 Ephesians 6:1–3	
Being Afraid	Deuteronomy 31:6–8 Joshua 1:7–9 Matthew 14:22–33	
Choosing Good or Evil	Deuteronomy 30:11–20 Psalm 1	
Who Is God?	Psalm 19	
The Shepherd Psalm	Psalm 23	
Trusting God	Psalm 37:3–8 Proverbs 3:3–6	
God Is with Us	Psalm 46	
Praising God	Psalm 100 Psalm 150	
The Importance of God's Law	Psalm 119:1–16 Psalm 119:33–48	
God's Help	Psalm 121	
God's Call	Genesis 12:1–4 Exodus 3:1–10 1 Samuel 3:1–10 Acts 26:12–18	
Peace	Isaiah 26:1–4 Isaiah 55:12, 13 Philippians 4:4–9	

TOPIC	BIBLE CHAPTER AND VERSE	DATE COMPLETED
Giving to God	Matthew 6:1–4 2 Corinthians 9:6–8	
The Lord's Prayer	Matthew 6:9–13	
The Beatitudes	Matthew 5:1–12	
Parables: The Talents The Good Samaritan	Matthew 25:14–30 Luke 10:30–37	
Forgiving Others	Ephesians 4:25–32	
The Christmas Story	Luke 2:1–20	
The Easter Story	Luke 24:1–12	
Jesus Called Disciples	Matthew 4:18–22 Mark 3:13–19	
Healing the Blind Man	John 9:1–11	
Feeding the 5,000	John 6:1–21	
The Good News	Romans 10:9, 10 Ephesians 2:8, 9	
Free from Sin	Romans 8:1–11	
Love	1 Corinthians 13	
The Fruit of the Spirit	Galatians 5:22–26	
Armor of God	Ephesians 6:10–20	
The Race	Philippians 3:12–14	
The Tongue	James 3:1–12	
Fellowship with God	1 John 1	

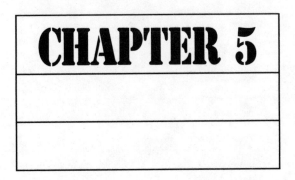

CHAPTER 5

Discover What

Ministers and Sunday school teachers are not the only people who can discover the meaning of Bible verses. You, too, can understand their meaning. Meditation is one way to do this. And, in the rest of this chapter, I will help you learn how to meditate. You can take my ideas and add your own to learn more from God.

You will need some books to help you. The first one is a Bible. I have been using the New King James Version in this book. Many people find it easier to memorize than some other versions. If you already have another version, you can use it or a family Bible.

The second book you need is a concordance or a Bible dictionary. Your family may already have

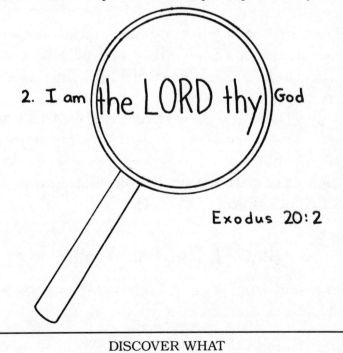

2. I am the LORD thy God

Exodus 20:2

a concordance like the *New Strong's Exhaustive Concordance of the Bible*. I used *Nelson's Illustrated Bible Dictionary* for the verse we are about to look up. A concordance is a book that gives you Bible verses that contain a certain word. This will help you find other places in the Bible that talk about the same thing as the verse or section you are studying. These books are difficult to use by yourself. You may need some help from your parents the first time you use them. Make sure your concordance refers to the version of the Bible you are using. If not, the word you're looking up might not be in there. Sometimes Bibles will have a dictionary, word list, or concordance in the back of the book. Check your Bible to see if it does.

The third book you need is a regular dictionary to be able to look up words you don't understand in the Bible dictionary or would like to know more about.

Again the three books you need for meditation are:

1. **A Bible**
2. **A concordance or a Bible dictionary**
3. **A dictionary**

Step #1: Find the Meaning

In discovering what a Bible verse is about, the first step is to know the meaning of the words.

Only look up the important words. *Of, a, are,* and *you* are nice words, but you probably already know their meaning. Even if you don't, they aren't as important as other words in your verse. You will not have time to research every word. Some verses will have one or two important words. Other verses will have many. Just because a verse has few important words does not mean that you shouldn't study the verse. Sometimes those simple verses can mean the most to you.

Use a Concordance and a Dictionary

You can find the meanings of words from Old Testament passages in the Hebrew dictionary at the back of a concordance and the meanings of words from New Testament passages in the Greek dictionary. When you are looking for the meanings of words in a concordance, first find the word in the front of the book. Then find the particular Scripture verse where the word appears. Next to the reference, you will find a number that refers you to the definition of the word in one of the dictionaries at the back of the book.

Before you look up words in a regular dictionary, find meanings in a Bible dictionary. Let's use our verse, Matthew 5:3, to do this:

> Blessed are the poor in spirit,
> For theirs is the kingdom of heaven.

I might decide to find the word *blessed* in the Bible dictionary. Looking under "B," just as if I were searching in the dictionary, I would try to find my word. In the *Nelson's Illustrated Bible Dictionary*, which I'm now using, *blessed* is not listed but *bless, blessing* is. As you can see in the close-up of the dictionary page shown below, several definitions are given under the word. Different verses in the Bible that use the word in other ways are included. Here's what the entry for

over the bed-chamber"—of Herod (Acts 12:20).

BLEACHER (see OCCUPATIONS AND TRADES).

BLEMISH (see DISABILITIES AND DEFORMITIES).

BLESS, BLESSING — the act of declaring, or wishing, God's favor and goodness upon others. The blessing is not only the good effect of words; it also has the power to bring them to pass. In the Bible, important persons blessed those with less power or influence. The patriarchs pronounced benefits upon their children, often near their own deaths (Gen. 49:1-28). Even if spoken by mistake, once a blessing was given it could not be taken back (Genesis 27).

Leaders often blessed people, especially when getting ready to leave them. These included Moses (Deuteronomy 33), Joshua (22:6-7), and Jesus (Luke 24:50). Equals could bless each other by being friendly (Gen. 12:3). One can also bless God, showing gratitude to Him (Deut. 8:10) in songs of praise (Ps. 103:1-2).

God also blesses people by giving life, riches, fruitfulness, or plenty (Gen. 1:22, 28). His greatest blessing is turning us from evil (Acts 3:25-26) and forgiving our sins (Rom. 4:7-8).

Cases of the opposite of blessing, or cursing, are often cited in the Bible (Deut. 27:11-26). Although

— 185 —

bless, blessing looks like in my Bible dictionary. Notice all the other Bible verses that are listed in the definition.

Get your index card with Matthew 5:3 again, and write under the verse the definition of *bless:* "The act of declaring or wishing God's favor and goodness upon others." You don't have to write the entire definition; just include enough to help you understand the meaning of the word.

After the definition, write the initials N.I.B.D. for *Nelson's Illustrated Bible Dictionary.* This will remind you where you found your definition, in case you want to look up the word again.

If your Bible dictionary includes other Scripture verses in the definition, you may want to look up these verses to see if they help you understand more about the words you are studying. You'll notice in the definition of *blessed* from my dictionary, *Nelson's Illustrated Bible Dictionary* (Nashville: Thomas Nelson, 1986), that there are several Scripture references. These refer to specific places in the Bible where either the word *bless* is used or where a blessing is being given.

If you still aren't clear about what *blessed* means, use your dictionary. You will need to look up *bless* again, because *blessed* probably won't be in there. Try to find a definition that matches the way the word is used in your verse. Write the definition on your card under the last sentence you wrote. Make sure that you put initials for your dictionary title next to the definition so you can find it again just like you did for the Bible dictionary.

You're doing great! You've just finished the front side of your card. You've done four of the six things that will be written on the card. Look at my card on this page. See if yours looks about the same. I didn't use a regular dictionary for this card, so yours may have more writing. It doesn't have to be exactly the same. But if it's close, you're on the right track.

Matthew 5:3
Blessed are the poor in spirit, For theirs is the kingdom of heaven.
Bless-(N.I.B.D., p.185) the act of declaring, or wishing God's favor and goodness upon others
Also read Matthew 5:10, 5:19 and 25:34

Where Else Can I Look?

If you want to read what someone else thought your verse meant, you could look it up in a book called a commentary. For our verse, you would need a commentary on the book of Matthew. Most families don't have commentaries on every book in the Bible at home. But most ministers do. You can ask your minister, or you can look in your church library. Some writers can be hard to understand, so have someone help you pick one that will be right for you. If you find something in the commentary that helps you understand the verse better, you could write this on the back of your card.

Now try these steps of meditation on the verse you chose after reading chapter 4. If you haven't already done so, write the book of the Bible, chapter number and verse in the upper left-hand corner of an index card. Copy the verse exactly the way it looks in your Bible. Pick out your key words, then look them up and write the definitions on the card. (Use the space below if you want to practice in the book.)

Pay attention to periods, commas, and other punctuation. They can help you understand verses. For instance, if the comma in Matthew 5:3

were after the word *poor* instead of *spirit*, the verse would seem to mean something else. It would sound as if the verse were talking about how much money the person had instead of how much he or she needed God. One other thing, don't skip over verses because you think they're boring. Sometimes these verses can be the most exciting, once they make sense.

Step #2: Ask God for Help

The second step is to ask God for understanding. Sometimes you may think, "What does this verse really mean?" Ask God. He doesn't mind. He wants you to ask. That's how you learn. When you don't understand something in school, what do you do? You ask your teacher, don't you? Well, God is the greatest teacher around. He wrote the textbook—the Bible—remember? Again, God probably won't say, "Now, Maria, Matthew 5:3 means . . ." Being still sometimes helps you discover answers you didn't think you knew. Or, He might bring someone into your life who can help answer your questions. Try asking your parents, or your minister, or a friend you trust.

To understand even more, ask yourself questions about the verse. Think about it. Talk to yourself as you think about the verses. Remember, to meditate means to talk quietly to yourself.

Pretend you're explaining your verse to a friend

or your brother or sister. If you have a pet, try talking to him or her about the verses. Your family may think you've gone crazy, but once they understand what you're doing, I'm sure they'll help. When you were very little, you talked to yourself all the time. It helped you to learn then. It can help you now.

Step #3: Say It Your Way

The third step is putting it in your own words. Put your name in the verse. After you have discovered the meaning of the more difficult words, rewrite the verse in words that are easier to understand. Put your name in the verse to make it more personal. For example, our verse, Matthew 5:3, might come out sounding like this:

Happy are you, Jennifer, because you know when you need God's help, for heaven is with you.

Some people like to do this for every verse they study. It helps them to feel like the Bible was written just for them. If you're one of those people, you could copy this verse in your own words on the back of your Matthew 5:3 card.

Once you've looked up all the words and gone through all the steps, then it's time to sit quietly with God. Sometimes, when we spend time with

God, we do all the talking. Have you ever had a friend that talked all the time, every time you were together? You probably had things you wanted to say, but you couldn't get a word in.

God wants a chance to talk to us, just as you want a chance to talk with your friend. That's why when you meditate, you should be listening more than talking. Think about what you've learned from your verse. Give God a chance to put the pieces of its meaning together for you just like a puzzle. Remember, find a quiet place where you and God can be alone together.

When you are ready to meditate, lie down on your bed. (Go ahead, try it. I dare you.) You can think best when you are comfortable. Make sure

your radio or tape player is off and that the room is quiet. Relax completely. Start by breathing deeply. When you are completely relaxed, begin to think about God and the Bible verse you are memorizing. Think about all those key words you've looked up and what they mean to you. Think about the words you changed to put the verse into words you could understand. It's amazing what you can learn when you are still and quiet with God!

Now that you know how to meditate, you can use this in the next chapter where you can think about what this verse means in your life.

CHAPTER 6

Draw Out Why

Drawing out why the verse we're studying is important in our lives is the hardest skill to practice. Sometimes it is very hard because what God is asking us to do may be different from what we would like to do. One day, my verse for memorizing was Ephesians 4:32: "And be kind to one another, tenderhearted, forgiving one another, just as God in Christ also forgave you." I was very angry at a friend of mine. After I read the verse, I knew that God wanted me to forgive that friend, even though I was mad.

Sometimes you will have a happy verse to memorize like Luke 2:14: "Glory to God in the highest, And on earth peace, good will toward men!" And something good will happen that day that makes you want to shout the verse out loud. The good thing about meditating is that the longer I think about what God wants me to do, I begin to want to do it.

There are three things to remember to make the Bible real for you: Use it every day; speak the verse when you need it; remember that the stories are real.

Use the Bible Every Day

I like to start the day memorizing and meditating on a new Bible verse. I think about how this verse might be important to me. Sometimes I take a walk with God in the morning and think about my verse. I look for signs of the verse in the world around me and in my own life. If you walk to school, you might want to try that, too. If you take the bus, maybe you could take a ride with God. I'm finding out that my day just isn't right without this special morning time. If you think better in the afternoon or evening, those could be your times with God. You could think about what happened that day. How did God speak to you on the playground? In the classroom? At home?

Say the Verses When You Need Them

You may experience some "close calls" in your life. You may come close to having an accident; someone may hurt your feelings; you may feel scared or lonely. You can feel God with you, keeping you safe in these times. You can hear Him talking to you through His Word.

At other times, you may be so full of joy that you want to tell everybody how you feel. Think of your mind as a computer. When you practice memorization and meditation, you are giving your mind input. When you need Him the most, God will help you get the verse from your memory bank that will be just what you need to hear.

When the devil tempted Jesus in the desert, what did Jesus do? Did He stick out His tongue and call the devil names? Did He run away and hide? No, He remembered verses He had memo-

rized as a child and used them to help Him through that hard time.

When you are asked to do something wrong you, too, can remember Bible verses, as long as you have taken the time to memorize and meditate on them. If someone asks you to steal something, you might use Exodus 20:15, "You shall not steal," to help you not steal. If your mother said you could stay overnight with your best friend, you might want to "Make a joyful shout to the Lord" (Psalm 100:1).

Remember the Stories Are Real

Try to think of John or Luke as your friend, telling you the story of another friend, Jesus. At Christmastime, memorize and meditate on the Christmas story. At Easter, look to the resurrection story to make that season come alive for you. The reason there are so many names and dates and places that are hard to say in the Bible is that the author of that book wanted you to know that the story was real. The Bible doesn't begin "Once upon a time . . ." like a fairy tale. It also doesn't end "And they lived happily ever after." These were real people who had real-life problems and, with God's help, they made it through.

If you're reading a confusing section, sometimes asking yourself questions as you study can help you learn more. Maybe your parent or friend could make up some questions. For example, as you study the Beatitudes, you may ask yourself, Who was Jesus talking to? What is a Beatitude? Why did Jesus make all of these statements? Which one of the Beatitudes is most like me? Which one would I like to be? What Beatitude might Jesus add if He were saying these today?

Once you've asked these questions, use the books you learned about in chapter 5, or go to someone you think could help you find the answers to your questions. Your parents or minister or Sunday school teacher may be able to help. They may not know the answers to your questions, but God can speak through them to help you find those answers.

Make Jesus your best friend. Tell Him all the things you would tell a friend about what is going on in your life and how much you care for Him. Then, look for His answers both in the Bible and in your life. When you discover some of these answers, you might want to write them on your index card. That way, they're always with you.

Now, you are ready to try this on your own. Let me give you a few more tips to help you begin and continue to memorize and meditate.

CHAPTER 7

Do It

Take a minute to remember the D's you've learned so far in this book:

Decide How

Determine Where

Discover What

Draw Out Why

Now it's time to *Do It*. How? Here are some helps:

1. **Schedule**
2. **Pray**
3. **Relax**
4. **Think Positive**

Schedule

Make time each day for the Bible. Talk to your parents. Find a time of day when you are almost always at home. It is important to set this time aside for God. Sometimes you have to make choices about what is really important. Maybe this could be a time when the whole family studies the Bible. Each person can memorize his own verses of Scripture. You could follow with a family talk time where each person shares what they've learned.

Pray

There are many times you can pray while you're doing it. Pray before you start to help you get still. Be quiet before God. If you work on a verse for a long time and can't seem to make sense of it, pray. Say something like: "God, I know You're trying to tell me something, but I don't know what it is." He won't get mad at you, but He will give you some help. You may not get the answers now but that's all right. God will give you the answers when the time is right.

Relax

You should be enjoying this time with God. If not, something is wrong. Don't push yourself to learn too many verses too fast. If your parents want you to learn more quickly, talk to them about your feelings. This should be a fun time for the whole family. Don't forget about those recess times! Your mind needs a break every once in a while.

Think Positive

Say, "I can." When you say "I can't!" you can't. Here is a Bible verse to memorize that will help you when you're stuck.

I can do all things through Christ who strengthens me.

Philippians 4:13

This doesn't mean we should brag to others about how many Bible verses we've memorized. Friends don't like to hear things like that. They'll "see" the verses by how your life changes as you become the person God wants you to be.

Let me give you a word I'll call "The Big C"— *Consistency*. This means you need to keep memorizing and meditating those verses even when you don't feel like it. Here are three C's to help you:

1. **Carry your cards.**
2. **Continue to review.**
3. **Call on a buddy.**

Carry Your Cards

You should have at least one complete index card by now. On the next page you will see what mine looked like when it was done.

Set Your Goals

Decide each week how many verses you will be able to learn. If you have a busy week, choose only a few verses. If your calendar is blank, choose more verses. If you think your week is free, and then Mom tells you Aunt Ernestine is coming to visit, or the coach calls four extra practices, or your music teacher tells you that you're playing for the Queen of England, don't give up. Just do the verses you missed next week. If all

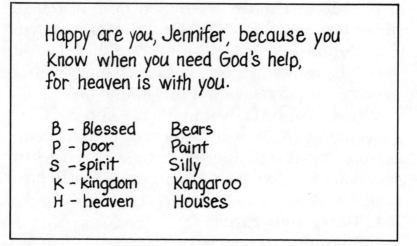

Happy are you, Jennifer, because you
Know when you need God's help,
for heaven is with you.

B - Blessed   Bears
P - poor   Paint
S - spirit   Silly
K - kingdom   Kangaroo
H - heaven   Houses

your weeks become busy, it may be time to sit down with your parents and talk about what is important to you.

Set goals that you can do. Don't try to do twenty verses in one week. Pick a number that you can easily work on and be able to remember. Usually one to three verses are plenty. This is not a race. If your brother or sister is memorizing five verses a week, it doesn't mean you have to memorize five verses. It's more important that you finish the goal you've set for yourself than try to learn the same as or more verses than anyone else.

Keep the verses you are studying someplace where you can see them. How about the refrigerator? If you have a bulletin board in your room, that's a good place too. If you have a younger brother or sister who might pull the cards down, or put sticky candy on them, or color all over them, you may want to put a plastic sandwich bag over them for protection. Once you've memorized that section, put your cards in your file box, so you can review them at another time.

Imagine yourself traveling from Seattle to Boston. This trip is about 3,000 miles. At first, that sounds like a lot, but when you break down the distance into what you will travel each day, it looks easier. Think of the goals you set each week like the towns that you will stay in each night of your trip. As you come to each town, you will be closer to finishing your journey. As you finish

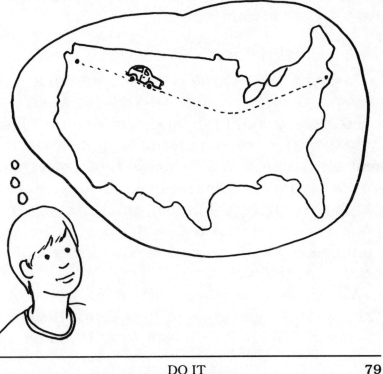

each goal, you are getting closer to the end of your trip. Before you know it, you've reached the end, memorizing the verses you have chosen from the Bible. You can enter the date you complete the verses in your "trip" in chapter 4.

If you need to break your trip down even further, use the schedule on page 81 to help you memorize and meditate each week for as little as fifteen minutes a day.

Remember, you don't have to follow this schedule exactly. Find what works for you. Just make sure that you give yourself time to listen to God, write out the cards, and review. This schedule could start on any day of the week. Choose what works best for your family.

Use a Card Holder

Carrying your cards with you can give you some extra practice time. This doesn't mean you need to carry your file box wherever you go. Take only the cards you're working on and maybe the rest of that section for review. Find something you already have that will hold those cards. Maybe you have a billfold, small purse, or a pocket calendar that the cards could fit in. You could make a holder out of an envelope or a sheet of construction paper.

Why carry your cards with you? If you're sitting around waiting to be picked up, they're a good way to make use of your time. If you have a

SUGGESTED WEEKLY GUIDE

1st Day—15 minutes
1. Start with prayer.
2. Write out one card.
3. Memorize first verse.
4. Read notes in your Bible for that verse.

2nd Day—15 minutes
1. Start with prayer.
2. Review yesterday's verse.
3. Look up unknown words.
4. Write what the verse means to your life.

3rd Day—15 minutes
1. Start with prayer.
2. Write out card for second verse.
3. Memorize second verse.
4. Read notes in your Bible for that verse.

4th Day—15 minutes
1. Start with prayer.
2. Review second verse.
3. Look up unknown words.
4. Write what the verse means to your life.

5th Day—15 minutes
1. Start with prayer.
2. If your goal was two verses, review the verses you learned and add them to your cards as needed. If your goal was three verses, write out the card for the next verse.

6th and 7th Days—
Rest and review the verses you've learned this week.

---

friend who's also memorizing and meditating, you could share your cards. Sometimes if you've had a really bad day, rereading your cards is like feeling God right there beside you.

Continue in Review

Make sure when you finish a section that you don't forget all about it. Go back and review once in a while. Think back to your trip. Reviewing a section you've already memorized is like looking at your pictures after you've come back from a vacation. It's reliving the trip all over again.

How often should you review? That depends on you—your schedule and how well you remember things. Perhaps your family could set aside a once-a-month or twice-a-month review session. Everyone in the family could review their cards and then share what they've learned.

Call on Your Buddy

Choose one person in your family or a close friend to be your study buddy. This should be someone you are able to talk to at least once a week. Make sure that the person you choose will get excited when you've reached your goal. Ask your buddy to hold your cards for the week and listen to you say your verses. Then you can do the same thing for your buddy. If you've just finished

a section of the Bible, see if you can quote the whole section. You might also spend your time sharing anything that you've learned about your verses this week that was especially important to you. Make sure you give your buddy a chance to share too.

Be careful to set aside this time to talk only about the Bible and your verses. Don't get sidetracked into telling your problems this week at school or talking about the new kid that just moved in. This can waste very special time together.

After you have recited your verses, tell each other the corrections you need to make. Be kind. Tell your buddy in a positive way the changes that need to be made.

Remember, you are not in a race with your buddy. Don't be upset if your buddy has more verses to say than you do. You're each taking your own trip. Go at your own pace.

Be faithful to your buddy. Don't say you can't meet with him/her unless it is an emergency. If this is the case, set up another time when you can meet as soon as possible.

Finally, pray for each other. Memorizing and meditating is not easy. Having a buddy will help you reach the end of your trip. If you're able, pray during your time together.

All of these three C's are for one purpose, The Big "C": *Consistency.* They are to help you successfully continue your learning.

One day on a beach in Hawaii, I saw a father teaching his son to surf. The father guided the back of his son's surfboard as he bent down and spoke instructions right into his son's ear. He showed the boy how to watch for just the right waves and told him exactly when to stand up.

As the waves rose James, the son, got into position and began to paddle. He waved at his dad, grinned, and stood up. But the boy fell. Just as he was going under, his dad was right there. He reached down into the waves and carefully placed the boy back onto the surfboard. Then, he told his son to listen again so he could learn to balance. He listened carefully to his father. Soon he was successful at surfing.

When you memorize and meditate, you can hear your heavenly Father give you instructions for your life. He will tell you what to do. If you listen to your heavenly Father, He will help you not to make mistakes. When you fall and get hurt, your Father will be there to rescue you. God will help you get over disappointments. And He will teach you about Himself.

Remember the acronym from page 38? Let's use those letters "B," "P," "S," "K," and "H" to make a new sentence to encourage you to be consistent with Memorize and Meditate:

Buddies Practicing Scriptures Know Him.

Have fun getting to know God!

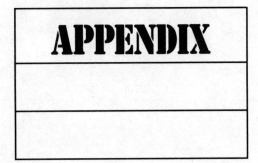

APPENDIX

Suggested Scriptures
for Memorize and Meditate

You can choose Scriptures from the following lists that are especially good for your age group.

AGES 2 TO 5

The First Rainbow	Genesis 9:8–17
The Ten Commandments	Exodus 20:1–17
	Ephesians 6:1–3
The Greatest Commandment	Deuteronomy 6:1–9
Choosing Good over Evil	Joshua 24:14–18
God's Call	1 Samuel 3:1–10
The Good and the Bad	Psalm 1
The Shepherd Psalm	Psalm 23
Praising God	Psalms 100; 150
God's Help	Psalm 121
Giving to God	Malachi 3:8–12
The Beatitudes	Matthew 5:1–12
The Lord's Prayer	Matthew 6:9–13
The Birth of Christ	Luke 2:1–20
The Resurrection	Luke 24:1–12
The New Birth	Romans 10:9–10
	Ephesians 2:8–9
Walking in the Spirit	Galatians 5:22–26
Forgiving Others	Ephesians 4:25–32
Armor of God	Ephesians 6:10–20
Right Thinking	Philippians 4:4–9

AGES 6 TO 12

History of Creation	Genesis 1—2
The First Rainbow	Genesis 9:8–17
God's Call	Genesis 12:1–4 Exodus 3:1–10 1 Samuel 3:1–10 Acts 26:12–18
The Ten Commandments	Exodus 20:1–17 Matthew 22:36–40 John 13:34–35 Ephesians 6:1–3
The Greatest Commandment	Deuteronomy 6:1–9
Choosing Good over Evil	Deuteronomy 30:11–20 Joshua 24:14–18
Encouragement	Deuteronomy 31:6–8 Isaiah 41:8–13 Matthew 14:22–33
Success	Joshua 1:7–9 Psalm 1
Obedience	1 Samuel 15:22–23 Matthew 7:21–23
The Good and the Bad	Psalm 1
Who Is God?	Psalm 19
The Shepherd Psalm	Psalm 23
Trusting God	Psalms 37:3–8; 118:5–9 Proverbs 3:3–6
Security in God	Psalm 46
Praising God	Psalms 100; 150
The Excellent Word of God	Psalm 119:1–16, 33–48

God's Help	Psalm 121
Sowing and Reaping	Psalm 126:4–6 Luke 8:4–18 Galatians 6:6–10
Peace	Isaiah 26:1–4; 55:11–13 Philippians 4:4–9
Daniel's Obedience to God	Daniel 1:6–21
Giving to God	Malachi 3:8–12 Matthew 6:1–4 2 Corinthians 9:6–8
Jesus Called Disciples	Matthew 4:18–22 Mark 3:13–19 Luke 5:1–11
The Beatitudes	Matthew 5:1–12
The Lord's Prayer	Matthew 6:9–13
Parables: The Talents The Good Samaritan	Matthew 25:14–30 Luke 10:30–37
Forgiving Others	Mark 11:25–26 Luke 17:1–4 Ephesians 4:25–32
The Birth of Jesus	Luke 2:1–20
The Resurrection	Luke 24:1–12
Miracle of Jesus	John 6:1–21
Healing Miracle of Jesus	John 9:1–11
Free from Sin	Romans 8:1–11
The New Birth	Romans 10:9–10 Ephesians 2:8–9
Love	1 Corinthians 13
Walking in the Spirit	Galatians 5:22–26
Armor of God	Ephesians 6:10–20
Right Thinking	Philippians 4:4–9

| The Tongue | James 3:1–12 |
| Fellowship with God | 1 John 1 |

AGES 13 TO 18

History of Creation	Genesis 1—2
The Fall of Man	Genesis 3
Noah, the Ark, the Flood	Genesis 6—8
The First Rainbow	Genesis 9:8–17
God's Call	Genesis 12:1–4 Exodus 3:1–10 1 Samuel 3:1–10 Acts 26:12–18
The Ten Commandments	Exodus 20:1–17 Matthew 22:36–40 John 13:34–35 Ephesians 6:1–3
The Greatest Commandment	Deuteronomy 6:1–9
Choosing Good over Evil	Deuteronomy 30:11–20 Joshua 24:14–18
Encouragement	Deuteronomy 31:6–8 Isaiah 41:8–13 Matthew 14:22–32
Success	Joshua 1:7–9 Psalm 1
The Walls of Jericho	Joshua 6
Obedience	1 Samuel 15:22–23 Matthew 7:21–23
David and Goliath	1 Samuel 17:32–50
The Good and the Bad	Psalm 1

Giving to God	Malachi 3:8–12
	Matthew 6:1–4
	2 Corinthians 9:6–8
Jesus Called Disciples	Matthew 4:18–22
	Mark 3:13–19
	Luke 5:1–11
The Sermon on the Mount	Matthew 5—7
The Lord's Prayer	Matthew 6:9–13
	John 17
Parables: The Tares, The Sheep and Goats, The Sower	Matthew 13:24–30, 36–43; 25:31–46 Luke 8:4–18
Parables: The Treasure, The Pearl, The Sheep, The Coin, The Son	Matthew 13:44; 13:45–46 Luke 15:4–7; 15:8–10; 15:11–32
The Day of the Lord	Matthew 24:36–44 1 Thessalonians 4:13—5:11
Parables: The Talents The Good Samaritan	Matthew 25:14–30; Luke 10:30–37
Healing Miracles of Jesus	Mark 5:21–43 Luke 5:17–25 John 2:1–12 John 9:1–11
Discipleship	Mark 8:34–38 Luke 14:26–33 John 8:31–36; 15:1–8
Prayer of Faith	Mark 11:22–26 John 12: 12–13 James 1:2–8; 5:13–18

Forgiving Others	Mark 11:25–26
	Luke 17:1–4
	Ephesians 4:25–32
The Birth and Resurrection of Christ	Luke 2:1–20
	Luke 24
Miracles of Jesus	John 2:1–12
	John 6:1–21
The New Birth	John 3:1–21
	Romans 10:1–17
	Ephesians 2:1–10
The Good Shepherd	John 10:1–15, 22–30
Death and Resurrection of Lazarus	John 11:1–44
Peace	John 14
Abiding in Christ	John 15:1–17
The Holy Spirit	Acts 1:4–8; 2:1–13
Justified by Faith	Romans 4
Christ's Love	Romans 5
Free from Sin	Romans 8
Spiritual Gifts	Romans 12
Freedom in Christ	Romans 14
Gifts and Diversities	1 Corinthians 12
Love	1 Corinthians 13
Walking in the Spirit	Galatians 5:16–26
Walk in Love, Light, and Wisdom	Ephesians 5:1–21
Armor of God	Ephesians 6:1–20
Humility	Philippians 2:1–24
Right Thinking	Philippians 4
Youth in Ministry	1 Timothy 4

Matthew 5:8
Blessed are the pure in heart,
For they shall see God.

Matthew 5:9
Blessed are the peacemakers,
For they shall be called sons of God.

Matthew 5:10
Blessed are those who are persecuted for righteousness'
sake,
For theirs is the kingdom of heaven.

Matthew 5:11

Blessed are you when they revile and persecute you, and say all kinds of evil against you falsely for My sake.

Matthew 5:12

Rejoice and be exceedingly glad, for great is your reward in heaven, for so they persecuted the prophets who were before you.

Matthew 5:13

You are the salt of the earth; but if the salt loses its flavor, how shall it be seasoned? It is then good for nothing but to be thrown out and trampled under foot by men.